Science Alive!
SOUND

CRABTREE
Publishing Company
www.crabtreebooks.com

How to use this book

Each chapter begins with experiments, followed by the explanation of the scientific concepts used in the experiments. Each experiment is graded according to its difficulty level. A level 4 or 5 means adult assistance is advised. Difficult words are in boldface and explained in the glossary on page 32.

Crabtree Publishing
www.crabtreebooks.com

PMB 16A, 350 Fifth Avenue,
Suite 3308, New York
New York 10118

612 Welland Avenue,
St. Catharines, Ontario,
Canada L2M 5V6

**Published in 2002
by Crabtree Publishing Company**

Published with Times Editions
Copyright © 2002 by Times Media Private Limited

Series originated and designed by
TIMES EDITIONS
An imprint of Times Media Private Limited
A member of the Times Publishing Group

Coordinating Editor: Ellen Rodger
Project Editors: P. A. Finlay, Carrie Gleason
Production Coordinator: Rosie Gowsell
Series Writers: Darlene Lauw, Lim Cheng Puay
Series Editor: Oh Hwee Yen
Series Designers: Loo Chuan Ming, Jailani Basari
Series Illustrator: Roy Chan Yoon Loy
Series Picture Researcher: Susan Jane Manuel

Cataloging-in-Publication Data
Lauw, Darlene.
    Sound / Darlene Lauw & Lim Cheng Puay.
        p. cm. — (Science alive)
    Includes index
    Summary: Presents activities that demonstrate how sound, especially musical sound, works in our everyday lives. History boxes feature the scientists who made significant discoveries in the field of sound.
    ISBN 0-7787-0562-5 (RLB) — ISBN 0-7787-0608-7 (pbk.)
    1. Sound—Experiments—Juvenile literature. [1. Sound—Experiments.
2. Music—Experiments. 3. Experiments.] I. Lim, Cheng Puay. II. Title.
    QC225.5 .L38 2002
    534'.078—dc21

                                                    2001042426
                                                    LC

Picture Credits
Marc Crabtree: cover; Bes Stock: 1, 10, 15 (bottom), 31 (top); Photobank Photolibrary Singapore: 19 (bottom); Science Photo Library: 7 (top, middle), 15 (top), 18 (top, bottom), 19 (top), 22 (bottom), 23, 26, 27 (top, middle); Travel Ink: 7 (bottom), 14; Trip Photo Library: 6, 11 (bottom), 22 (top), 30, 31 (middle)

Printed and bound in Malaysia
2 3 4 5 6—0S—07 06 05 04 03

INTRODUCTION

We are constantly surrounded by sounds such as the chirping of birds, the roar of traffic, and people talking. Musicians arrange sound in a way that is pleasing to the ear. Doctors use sound to treat their patients. Sound occurs when an object vibrates. These vibrations travel through the air and reach our ears. Learn more about sound by reading and doing fun experiments.

Contents

Sound energy *4*

Transmission of sound *8*

The speed of sound *12*

Hearing sound *16*

Playing with sound waves *20*

Qualities of sound *24*

Fun with music *28*

Glossary and index *32*

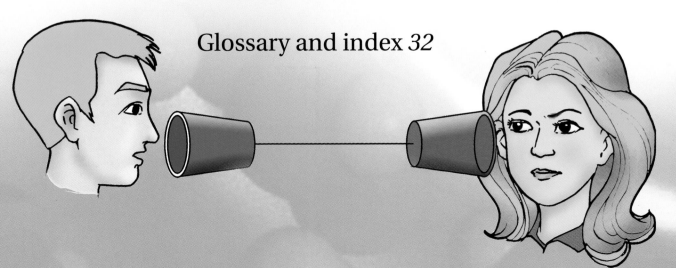

Sound energy

S ound is a form of **energy**. We hear it and can feel it when we stand near speakers at a concert. You can actually "see" sound energy too.

Seeing sound!

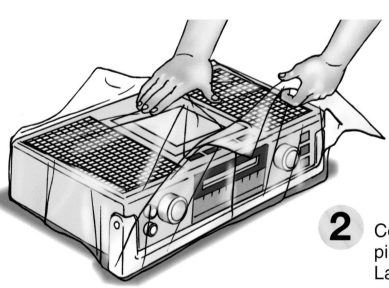

1 Cut out a piece of plastic wrap. Make sure that the piece you cut is big enough to cover the entire radio.

2 Cover the radio with the piece of plastic wrap. Lay the radio on its back, so that the speakers face upward.

3 Put on the protective eyewear. Sprinkle some sand over the plastic wrap and turn on the radio. Slowly turn up the volume. Do you see the sand jumping?

4

Sound travels in waves. Here is a simple model to show how sound energy moves. All you need is a slinky toy.

Difficult — 5
— 4
Moderate — 3
— 2
Easy — 1

You will need:
- A slinky toy
- Two friends

Sound waves

1 Lay the slinky toy on the floor. Ask your friends to hold both ends of the slinky toy. Extend the slinky toy until it is as straight as it can be.

2 Now, hold the center portion of the slinky toy and move it first to the left, then to the right. The coils in different parts of the slinky toy are squeezed together at some times and stretched out at other times.

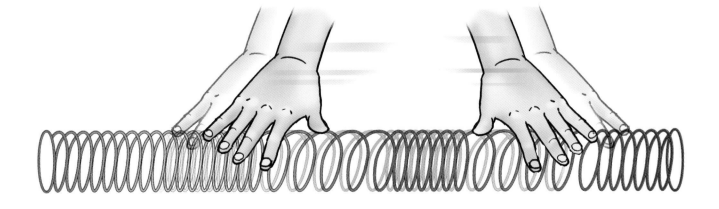

5

Sound moves!

Sound is a form of energy that is produced when an object vibrates or moves. The vibrating object sends out energy in the form of **longitudinal waves**. These waves travel through a **medium**, such as air, to reach our ears. In the experiment *Seeing Sound*, sound energy traveled from the radio through the surrounding air to the sand, causing the air and the sand to vibrate. These vibrations made the sand "jump."

Waves are created when the **molecules** of an object move. For example, if you bang on a steel pot, you will cause the steel to vibrate. These vibrations cause the molecules in the air surrounding the pot to cram together, then move away from each other, creating waves. In the *Sound Waves* experiment, the movement of the slinky toy was similar to the waves of molecules that are caused by sound vibrations.

Moving molecules that create sound waves are like messengers that carry sound from vibrating objects to our ears. What would happen if the air had fewer molecules? Would sound still reach our ears?

There is very little air on the moon and, therefore, fewer molecules for sound to travel through. Sound travels very poorly in such an environment. Astronauts use microphones and radios to communicate with one another on the moon.

Robert Boyle

Robert Boyle (1627–1691), an English scientist, was the first to show that sound cannot travel through a **vacuum**. To do this, he hung a bell by a string in a glass jar. Then, using an air pump, he created a vacuum by sucking the air out of the jar. While he was doing that, he rang the bell. As more air was released from the jar, the sound from the bell became softer and softer. When there was no air left in the jar, the bell made no sound.

Did you know?

A stethoscope is a medical instrument consisting of a bell and a **diaphragm** connected to a rubber tube. The French doctor Rene Theophile Hyacinthe Laennec invented this device in 1816. Since then, doctors have been using stethoscopes to listen to the sounds our internal organs make. This helps them check if our organs are functioning properly.

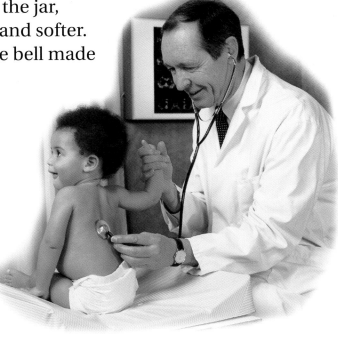

SLEEPING SOUNDLY

The World Health Organization recommends that the noise level during sleep should only be around 30 dBs (**decibels**). This is the noise level in a quiet library (*left*). You may not be able to sleep well if your bedroom is noisier than that.

Transmission of sound

Some cartoons show hunters with one ear on the forest ground, listening for the footsteps of nearby animals. Try this experiment to see if this method really works.

You will need:
- A table
- A friend
- A coin

The ear on the table

1 Stand at one end of the table. Ask your friend to stand at the other end.

2 Have your friend tap the coin on the table. Can you hear the tapping?

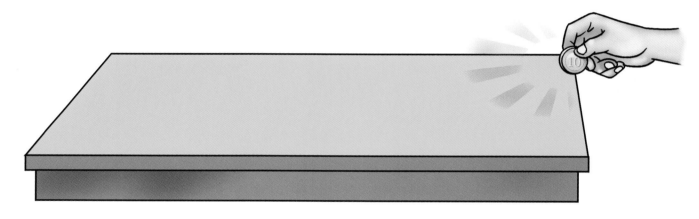

3 Now, place your ear on the tabletop. Ask your friend to tap the table with the coin again. Is the tapping louder now?

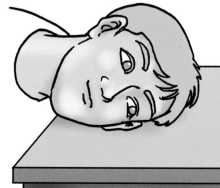

You need to pass a secret message to your friend in a hurry. You cannot whisper because your friend is too far away from you. What can you do?

Difficult – 5
– 4
Moderate – 3
– 2
Easy – 1

You will need:
• Two paper cups
• A friend
• A ballpoint pen
• A piece of string 10 feet (3 m) long
• Tape

Spy telephone

 1 Hold a cup in your hand and ask your friend to do the same. Stand 10 feet (3 m) away from your friend.

2 Ask your friend to put the other cup over his or her ear. Whisper into your cup. Can your friend hear you?

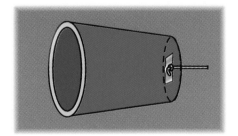

3 Now, use the point of the pen to make a small hole on the bottom of each cup. Pull one end of the string through the hole of one cup and tie a knot inside the cup. Tape the knot to the bottom of the cup.

4 Ask your friend to do the same with the other end of the string and the other cup.

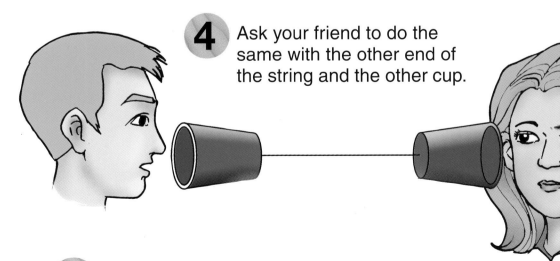

5 Now, walk away from your friend until the string is pulled tight. Whisper into your cup. Can your friend hear you with the other cup?

9

Transmission of sound

Molecules **transmit** sound when they vibrate in the material sound is passing through. This material, or medium, is known as a conductor of sound. Sound travels better through a medium with tightly packed molecules. The molecules in a solid medium are arranged closer than in a gaseous or liquid medium. This is why solids are the best conductors of sound. Gases such as air are the poorest conductors of sound because they have fewer molecules, and the molecules are spread far apart. Tables and strings are both examples of solids. Now you know why the tapping of the coin was louder when you placed your ear on the tabletop, and why you could hear your friend better through the spy telephone.

Instead of using paper cups for your spy telephone, you can use cans. These will work just as well. But beware of the sharp edges!

Sir Isaac Newton

Isaac Newton (1642–1727) was the first to find out that there is a relationship between sound transmission and the way molecules are packed in the medium. The famous British mathematician and physicist was also the first to explain this discovery to the world.

Did you know?

Pay attention to how you sound the next time you record your voice on tape or video. Is the **pitch** of your voice higher than usual? This is because the sound waves from your **vocal cords** have to pass through your bones and body fluids to reach your ears. This lowers the pitch of your voice. To hear what your friends sound like to themselves, place your ear on their backs and listen while they speak.

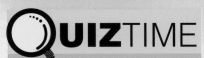

QUIZTIME

If solid objects are the best sound conductors, why do some people use earplugs to block out sound?

Answer: Some solid materials, such as cork, rubber, and cotton, are poorer conductors of sound than others. If we examine these materials, we will find many air pockets inside them. The air pockets make them good absorbers of sound.

THE SOUND OF SILENCE

Musicians record their music in soundproof rooms. The walls of a soundproof room are padded with sound absorbers. People outside the room will not be able to hear the sounds produced inside. Similarly, sounds outside will not enter the room. Soundproof rooms allow musicians to record music without interference from sounds outside the rooms.

The speed of sound

S ound travels through air at a speed of 1,083 feet per second (330 m per second), or nearly 738 miles per hour (1,188 km per hour). It is easy to calculate the speed of sound. You can do it yourself!

Difficult – 5
– 4
Moderate – 3
– 2
Easy – 1

You will need:
- A measuring tape
- A brick or stone wall
- A friend
- A stopwatch
- Two metal rods

Calculating the speed of sound

1 Using the measuring tape to guide you, stand 270 feet (82 m) from the wall with your friend. Ask your friend to hold the stopwatch while you hold the two metal rods.

2 Bang the rods together. At the same time, start the stopwatch. Listen for the echo. Your friend should stop the watch as soon as the echo is heard. Repeat this 20 times.

3 Multiply the distance to the wall and back (540 feet or 164 m) by the number of echoes you recorded (20 echoes). Divide the result by the total time the sound took to travel the distance, as noted on the stopwatch. You would probably have taken about 0.3 seconds to react to each echo before you recorded it. Subtract 20 X 0.3 seconds from your calculation to allow for your reaction time. The final figure will be the approximate speed of sound in feet per second!

$$\frac{540 \text{ feet (164 m) X 20}}{\text{Time} - 20 \text{ X } 0.3} = \text{Speed of sound (feet per second)}$$

Do you know why you often hear thunder after lightning flashes during a storm? The electrical charge of lightning produces heat. That heat causes air to expand suddenly, resulting in an explosion of air known as thunder. You will hear thunder about five seconds after you see lightning flash a mile (1.6 km) away. If lightning flashes 2 miles (3.2 km) away, you will hear thunder ten seconds later. By timing the interval between lightning flashes and thunder, you can estimate how far away storm clouds are from you.

Difficult — 5
— 4
Moderate — 3
— 2
Easy — 1

You will need:
- A stopwatch
- A pencil or pen
- A notebook

Tracking a storm

1 From inside your house, start the stopwatch when you see lightning flash. Stop it when you hear thunder. Record the time in the notebook.

2 To find out where the storm clouds are, divide the time difference between the lightning flash and the thunder by five. Record your calculations in the notebook.

3 Reset the stopwatch and repeat the procedure every time lightning flashes. The distances you calculate will tell you whether the storm is coming closer or moving farther away.

time delay / sec	km
	6
	5
30 sec	
25 sec	

The speed of sound is not always the same!

How fast sound travels depends on many things, including temperature. The speed of sound increases by about one foot per second (30.5 cm per second) for each degree Fahrenheit (0.55°C) rise. This is because molecules vibrate faster in warm than in cold air. When the molecules vibrate faster, sound waves can travel more quickly. For example, echoes take a longer time to bounce back in cold mountain ranges than in warm valleys.

Sound travels faster in warm places, such as the Grand Canyon, Arizona, than in cold places.

Marin Mersenne

Marin Mersenne (1588–1648), a French mathematician, was the first to measure the speed of sound. He did this by creating echoes and timing their return. Mersenne's estimated speed of sound was only ten percent off the actual speed.

Did you know?

The speed of sound also varies with the medium of transmission. Sound travels fastest in solids, slower in liquids, and slowest in gases. The speed of sound in steel is actually 16,400 feet per second (4,999 m per second), which is fifteen times faster than in air! Sound travels at a speed of around 20,000 feet per second (6,096 m per second) in glass, 4,658 feet per second (1,420 m per second) in water, and 3,041 feet per second (927 m per second) in helium.

SOUND AND GLOBAL WARMING

Many people think that the temperature of the oceans is rising due to global warming. Global warming occurs when the heat radiating from the Earth is trapped by gases in the Earth's **atmosphere**. How do you find out if the Earth is heating up? Scientists have thought of one way: by measuring the speed at which sound travels in the oceans. Sound would travel faster in a warmer ocean than in cooler waters. Regular monitoring of the speed of sound in oceans would inform us if they are getting hotter over time.

Hearing sound

Have you ever wondered how your ear works? How does it pick up sounds from your surroundings? This simple model of your ear will help you find out!

Artificial ear

You will need:
- A small pocketknife
- A styrofoam board
- Glue
- The cardboard tube from an empty toilet paper roll
- Tape
- A paper plate
- A piece of tracing paper
- Three elastic bands
- Four thumbtacks
- A small, thin wooden stick
- A paper cup
- Water
- A radio

1 Ask an adult to cut a base and two supports as shown in the diagram, using the pocketknife and the styrofoam board.

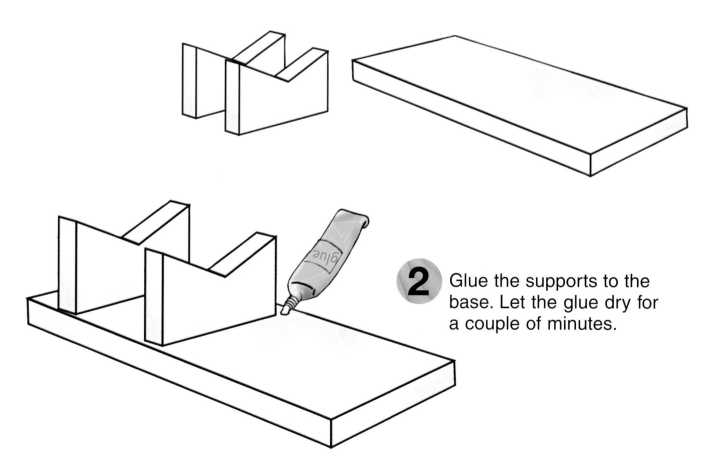

2 Glue the supports to the base. Let the glue dry for a couple of minutes.

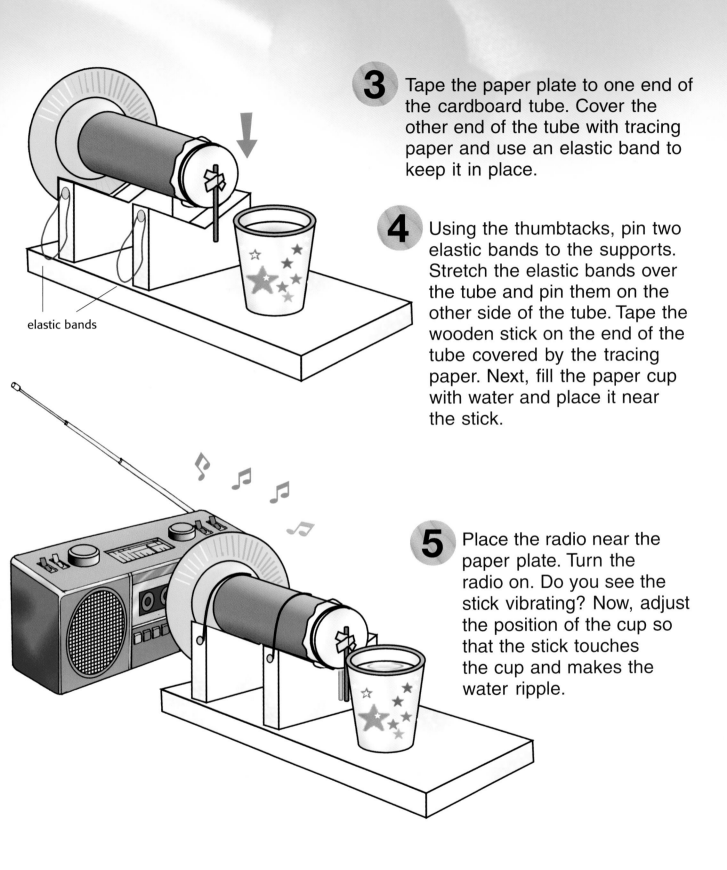

3 Tape the paper plate to one end of the cardboard tube. Cover the other end of the tube with tracing paper and use an elastic band to keep it in place.

4 Using the thumbtacks, pin two elastic bands to the supports. Stretch the elastic bands over the tube and pin them on the other side of the tube. Tape the wooden stick on the end of the tube covered by the tracing paper. Next, fill the paper cup with water and place it near the stick.

5 Place the radio near the paper plate. Turn the radio on. Do you see the stick vibrating? Now, adjust the position of the cup so that the stick touches the cup and makes the water ripple.

elastic bands

Inside the ear

The human ear consists of three parts: the outer ear, the middle ear, and the inner ear. The outer ear is the bony flap at the side of your head. It collects sound signals from its surroundings. In the experiment *Artificial Ear*, the paper plate behaved like the outer ear. The cardboard tube served the same function as the ear canal. It channels the sound waves the outer ear collects to the eardrum in the middle ear. The eardrum vibrates when it receives the sound, like the tracing paper did in the experiment. The vibration of the tracing paper caused the wooden stick to quiver. The stick represented the smallest bones in the human body. These bones are called the hammer, the anvil, and the stirrup. They are located in the middle ear. Their role is to transfer sound to the inner ear. In the experiment, the water in the cup represented the fluid in the inner ear. This fluid transmits the sound waves to tiny hairs called cilia. Cilia hairs send sound to the brain. The brain then translates the information into the sound we hear from the radio.

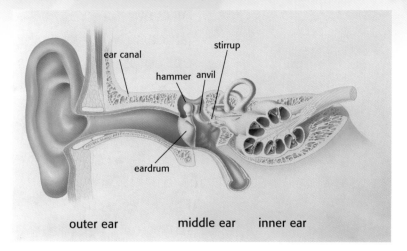

ear canal

stirrup

hammer anvil

eardrum

outer ear   middle ear   inner ear

When you cup your hand behind your ear, you are increasing the size of the outer ear. This helps your ear collect more sound. Cupping your hands behind your ears amplifies the sounds you hear by as much as ten decibels!

Can you hear me?

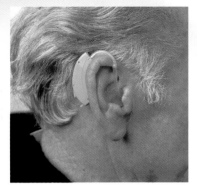

Hearing aids are devices that help people who are hard of hearing. These devices are placed inside or behind the ear to collect and amplify sound. Until the 1700s, people used bulls' horns, shell conches, and tin or rubber funnels as hearing aids. Modern hearing aids are powered by batteries and usually have three parts: a microphone, an amplifier, and a receiver. Each part has a special function. The amplifier helps to increase the volume of the sound the ear receives. The microphone changes the sound into electric signals. The receiver changes these signals back into sound. A small tube at the end of the receiver directs the amplified sound into the ear canal of the person who wears the hearing aid.

QUIZTIME

Which is louder? The sound of a train horn ten feet (30 m) away or a truck five feet (fifteen meters) away from you?

Answer: Both the horn and the truck make sounds as loud as 90–100 dBs. However, our ears tend to amplify sounds that are high in pitch. Therefore, you may think that the high-pitched horn is louder.

Did you know?

Different animals have different hearing ranges. Dogs can detect sounds that are too high-pitched for the human ear. Bats can hear sounds that are too low-pitched for humans to notice. The **frequency** of a sound wave determines its pitch. Pitch or frequency is measured in **hertz** (Hz). The list below shows the hearing ranges of humans and some other animals.

Animal	Hearing range (Hz)
Human	20–20 000 Hz
Bat	10–110 000 Hz
Dog	20–40 000 Hz
Dolphin	110–130 000 Hz

DEAFENING SOUND

We start to lose our hearing after eight hours of nonstop exposure to a noise level of 150 dBs. This is just ten decibels higher than a rocket launch, or 50 dBs louder than the sound a lawn mower makes.

Playing with sound waves

Difficult — 5
— 4
Moderate — 3
— 2
Easy — 1

You will need:
- Two umbrellas
- Aluminum foil
- A friend
- A watch or stopwatch that ticks

Y ou can collect sound waves with an umbrella. You can also turn an umbrella into a radar dish.

Collecting sound waves with an umbrella

1 Open the umbrellas. Line the insides of each umbrella with aluminum foil.

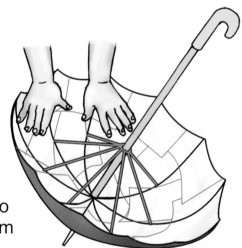

2 Pass one umbrella and the watch to your friend and ask your friend to stand about 10 feet (3 m) away from you. Point the handles of the umbrellas toward each other as shown in the diagram.

3 Ask your friend to put the stopwatch near the handle of the umbrella, as shown in the diagram. Now, place your ear near the center of your umbrella. Can you hear the stopwatch ticking?

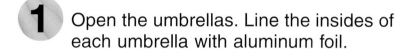

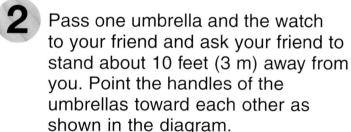

Echoes are sound waves reflected off surfaces. Learn more about echoes with this experiment.

Difficult — 5
— 4
Moderate — 3
— 2
Easy — 1

You will need:
• Two pieces of cardboard
• Tape
• Two friends
• An alarm clock that ticks
• A piece of string
• A protractor

Reflecting sound waves

1 Roll both pieces of cardboard into two tubes of equal sizes. Use the tape to secure the edges of the cardboard.

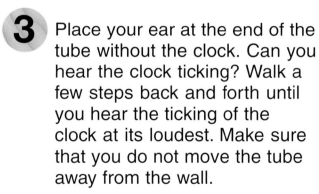

2 With one friend, position the two tubes against the wall as shown in the diagram. Hold the alarm clock at one end of one of the tubes.

3 Place your ear at the end of the tube without the clock. Can you hear the clock ticking? Walk a few steps back and forth until you hear the ticking of the clock at its loudest. Make sure that you do not move the tube away from the wall.

4 Then, ask your other friend to tape the string to the point where the two tubes meet. Extend the string and hold it perpendicular to the wall, at an angle of 90 degrees.

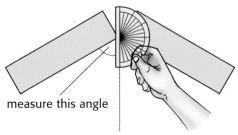

measure this angle

5 Use the protractor to measure the angle each tube makes with the string. Are the angles identical?

Bouncing off!

In the experiment with the umbrellas, you could hear the ticking of the stopwatch from a distance. That was because sound waves from the stopwatch were reflected from your friend's umbrella to your umbrella. The shape of the umbrella focused these sound waves toward the center, where your ear was.

The second experiment, *Reflecting Sound Waves*, showed that sound waves are reflected at the same angle they hit any surface. The ticking of the clock was loudest when the angles between both tubes and the string were identical.

Satellite dishes (*below*) work in the same way the umbrellas did in the experiment *Collecting Sound Waves with an Umbrella*. Satellite dishes in space collect wave energy before transmitting it to Earth. Satellite dishes placed on Earth receive the incoming wave energy.

Using echoes

Humans and animals use echoes to find things. For example, sailors use echoes to locate the seabed, shoals of fish, and submarines. They do this with the help of a sonar device. The sonar device sends out a pulse of sound. When the sound hits an object, it bounces back, or echoes. A microphone amplifies the echo. The sailors measure the time for the sound to travel to and from the ship. They then calculate the distance to the object.

Some animals, such as bats, also rely on echoes to find their way around and to hunt for food. Bats have very poor eyesight and cannot see in the dark. To help them "see" their surroundings, bats produce extremely high-pitched sounds, which bounce off the objects around them. The echoes returning to a bat's ears will tell the bat exactly how far away cave walls and prey, such as moths and beetles, are.

Have you ever heard the expression "blind as a bat?" Bats have very poor eyesight and are almost blind.

Did you know?

Ancient Greeks had a different way of explaining echoes. In Greek mythology, Echo was the name of a mountain nymph. One day, she assisted Zeus, the ruler of the Greek gods, in deceiving his wife, Hera. To punish her, Hera took away Echo's ability to speak her own words. Instead, she could only repeat the things other people said.

CAN YOU SHOUT LOUD ENOUGH?

If you ever have the chance to stand among snow-covered peaks, try to create echoes by shouting to the mountains! Some people believe that the noise you make can set off an avalanche. Is that true? Not unless you can make a sound as loud as 150 dBs, or as loud as a bomb going off at close range.

Qualities of sound

W hat happens to mediums when the sound passing through them gets louder and louder? Try this experiment to find out!

You will need:
- A balloon
- A radio

Dancing balloon!

1 Blow up the balloon until it is about three-quarters full.

2 Turn on the radio and place the balloon near one of the radio speakers.

3 Slowly increase the volume of the radio. Can you feel the balloon vibrating?

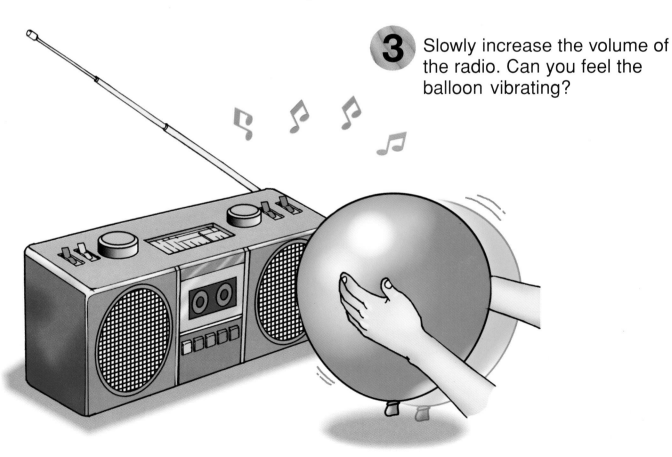

You have seen how sound travels in waves. You have also learned that sound waves can be pressed together, or compressed. What happens to the quality of sound when it is compressed?

Difficult — 5
— 4
Moderate — 3
— 2
Easy — 1

You will need:
- A friend
- A whistle
- A bicycle
- An open space to cycle fast

Squeezing sound waves

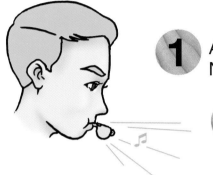

1 Ask your friend to blow the whistle. Note the pitch of its sound.

2 Ask your friend to take the bicycle and walk 33 feet (20 m) away from you. Tell your friend to prepare to cycle toward you. Your friend should not blow the whistle yet.

3 Signal to your friend to start cycling. Ask your friend to start blowing the whistle once he or she is about 16.5 feet (10 m) away, and to stop only when he or she has cycled past you. Note the pitch of the whistle as your friend cycles toward and past you.

Volume and pitch

Why did the balloon shake when you turned up the volume of the radio in the experiment *Dancing Balloon*? When you increased the noise from the radio, more sound energy was transmitted to the air molecules in the balloon. The molecules vibrated more vigorously and caused the balloon to shake.

Have you ever noticed that when an ambulance on the road passes by you, the pitch of its siren increases as it approaches you and decreases once it passes you? Sound waves in front of a moving object are compressed when it moves toward you. This compression of sound waves increases the frequency and makes the pitch higher. The sound waves behind the ambulance are stretched. As the sound waves become longer, they decrease in frequency and pitch. This change in sound frequency of a moving object is called the **Doppler Effect**. Now you know why the pitch of the whistle increased in the experiment *Squeezing Sound Waves* as your friend cycled toward you and decreased as he or she cycled past you!

The Doppler Effect is most noticeable when we listen to fast moving objects such as jets and racing cars. Jets carry Doppler radar to check their ground speed by bouncing waves off the ground.

Doppler's discovery

The Austrian physicist Christian Johann Doppler (1803–1853) was the first to describe the Doppler Effect. In 1845, he demonstrated the Doppler Effect using an experiment with two groups of trained musicians. Doppler placed one group along a railway track. The other group of musicians played trumpets on a train traveling very fast. The musicians along the track then noted the rise in pitch as the railway carriage came toward them and the fall in pitch as it sped away from them.

Did you know?

Have you ever wondered why fog horns always produce low-pitched sounds? This is because we can hear low-pitched sounds farther away than high-pitched sounds. Ships can hear the low-pitched warning of fog horns a long distance away. This gives them enough time and space to change their routes to avoid crashing into oncoming ships.

QUIZTIME

Can jets fly faster than the speed of sound?

Answer: Yes! Some jets fly at **supersonic** speeds. In supersonic flight, the air molecules in front of the jet cannot move away quickly enough to make way for the jet. As a result, the air is compressed. As the jet continues flying, the compressed air suddenly expands behind the nose of the jet. This creates a loud bang, known as **a sonic boom.**

A GROWING UNIVERSE?

The Doppler Effect also works for light, radio, and radar waves. Astronomers have used the Doppler Effect to study light waves in space. They have found that some distant stars have a red tinge around them (*above*). The red tinge shows that light is reaching the Earth from stars that are moving away from the planet. The light the stars emit is stretched. Could this mean that the Universe is expanding?

Fun with music

Pipes and flutes are wind instruments. Wind instruments use moving air to produce sound. Make your own wind instrument, a panpipe, using straws.

Difficult — 5
— 4
Moderate — 3
— 2
Easy — 1

You will need:
- Ten straws
- Scissors
- Tape

A straw panpipe

1 Squeeze and flatten one end of each straw. Cut it as shown in the diagram.

2 Lay the straws on a table next to one another in a straight line. Tape them together.

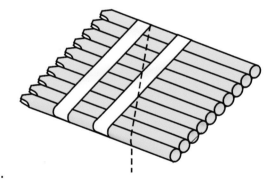

3 Cut the straws diagonally so that they are different lengths.

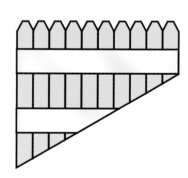

4 To play your pipes, simply blow across the ends!

You have made your own wind instrument. Now, learn how to make your own percussion instrument. Percussion instruments produce sounds when you strike them. The xylophone is an example of a percussion instrument.

Difficult — 5
— 4
Moderate — 3
— 2
Easy — 1

You will need:
- Eight glasses of the same shape. Four of these glasses must be smaller than the other four.
- A pencil
- A jug filled with water

Glass xylophone

1 Tap some glasses on their rims with the pencil. Choose glasses that give a clear tone when you strike them.

2 Fill one glass with a little water. This is glass number one. Strike it. Call the tone you hear *do*. The eight glasses should cover a musical range called an **octave**, which is made up of the eight tones *do-re-mi-fa-so-la-ti-do.* Always tune the bigger glasses first.

3 Sing the next tone of the octave (*re*). Tune the next glass to this tone by adding a little water at a time. Tap the glass as you pour in the water. Stop when you hear the right tone. This is glass number two.

4 Continue tuning the rest of the glasses until they produce the tones of the octave. Use the smaller glasses for the higher notes of the range.

5 Now, see if you can tap out a tune on the glasses. Try tapping the glasses in this order: 3-2-1-2-3-3-3. Do you know the tune?

Making music

Musicians make sound in wind instruments by vibrating the air in the tube or column of the instrument. In the experiment *A Straw Panpipe*, you heard a different pitch from each straw as you blew across your panpipe. The pitch depended on the length of each straw. Each straw had a different amount of air. The shorter the column, the higher the pitch. You can also get a range of tones using just one pipe. To do this, simply cut holes along the length of the straw. By opening and closing the holes, you are changing the length of the column of air!

Players of percussion instruments, or percussionists, produce sound in two main ways. They either make use of the vibration of the air trapped in the instruments or the vibration of the instruments themselves. By varying the sizes of drums, drummers cause different amounts of air to vibrate as they are playing. This lets them produce a variety of tones. In the *Glass Xylophone* experiment, we heard a range of tones because we varied the amount of air vibrating in each glass.

Guitarists produce different tones by pressing on the individual strings of the guitar. This adjusts the length of string that vibrates when they pluck it. A harmonica is like a panpipe. Its pitch varies according to the length of air in each column of the instrument.

When did music start?

In the Middle East, archaeologists have uncovered musical instruments that are more than 3,500 years old. From their finds, we know that drums and flutes were probably among the first instruments made. Most early instruments could not produce a wide range of tones. Some indigenous groups made simple instruments with limited ranges. The South American natives' nose flutes, for example, have only a few tones. The native people play the flutes by exhaling through their noses into the instruments!

QUIZTIME

Which pipe has a wider range of tones, one with more holes or one with fewer holes?

Answer: The pipe with more holes.

The bars of the xylophone are different lengths. The vibration of each bar produces a different tone.

Did you know?

You can shatter glass using just your voice! Glass, like most other mediums, has a **natural frequency**. If you sing at the pitch of this frequency, the sound of your voice will cause the molecules of glass to vibrate violently. As you sing louder, the vibration builds. It eventually exerts a force that is stronger than the bonds holding the molecular structure of the glass together. This causes the glass to shatter.

THAT RINGING IN YOUR EAR

Many people hear a ringing in their ears after they leave a rock concert. The ringing sound comes from the vibration of cilia hairs in the ear. Cilia hairs vibrate according to the loudness of the sound a person hears. As the sound gets louder, the vibration of the hairs increase. Sometimes, the hairs vibrate so much that they are damaged or even destroyed. Once that happens, people will start to lose their hearing permanently because cilia hairs do not grow back.

Glossary

atmosphere (page 15): The air surrounding the Earth and other planets.

decibel (page 7): The measurement of sound pressure.

diaphragm (page 7): A thin disk which vibrates when receiving sound waves.

Doppler Effect (page 26): A change in the frequency of waves from a moving source. An observer in a fixed position will notice the Doppler Effect either as a change in pitch or a distortion of light.

energy (page 4): A form of power.

frequency (page 19): The number of completed cycles a wave makes per unit of time. A wave makes a complete cycle when it experiences a period of compression and one of expansion.

hertz (page 19): A unit of frequency that one uses in the measurement of pitch.

longitudinal waves (page 6): Waves of energy that move in the same direction as the vibration of the particles in the medium.

medium (page 6): A substance through which energy acts.

molecule (page 6): The smallest unit of a substance that can exist by itself.

natural frequency (page 31): The frequency of a sound wave at which the vibration of the molecules in a medium is most violent.

octave (page 29): A series of eight tones (*do re mi fa so la ti do*) on a musical scale.

pitch (page 11): How high or low a tone is in music or sound.

sonic boom (page 27): A loud noise a supersonic aircraft makes when it travels faster than the speed of sound.

supersonic (page 27): Refers to speeds that are faster than the speed of sound.

transmit (page 10): To cause energy to pass through a medium.

vacuum (page 7): A space that is completely empty.

vocal cords (page 11): The part of the throat that vibrates as air from the lungs passes through. This vibration produces sound.

Index

absorbers of sound, 11

Boyle, Robert, 7

cilia hairs, 18, 31
conductors of sound, 10, 11

Doppler, Christian Johann, 27
Doppler Effect, 26, 27

echo, 12, 14, 15, 21, 22, 23,

hearing aids, 19
hearing range, 19
human ear, 18

Laennec, Rene
    Theophile Hyacinthe, 7
levels of disturbance, 7, 19

Mersenne, Marin, 15

Newton, Isaac, 10

sonar, 23
sound transmission, 8, 9, 10, 11,
    14, 15
sound waves, 5, 6
speed of sound, 12, 14, 15, 27

volume and pitch, 11, 19, 24, 26,
    27, 30, 31

wind instruments, 28, 30, 31
World Health Organization, 7

DIVE!

MY ADVENTURES IN THE DEEP FRONTIER

Sylvia A. Earle

Dive!

My Adventures In